GAS II

GEORG KAISER

GAS II

A Play in Three Acts

Introduction by
VICTOR LANGE
Princeton University

FREDERICK UNGAR PUBLISHING CO.
NEW YORK

Published by arrangement with
Verlag Kiepenhauer & Witsch, Köln

Translated by Winifred Katzin

Second Printing, 1972

Copyright 1963 by
Frederick Ungar Publishing Co., Inc.

Printed in the United States of America

ISBN 0-8044-6344-1
Library of Congress Catalog Card No. 63-14962

INTRODUCTION

THE CHANGES in feeling and perception that began
to take shape among the poets and painters at the
turn of this century, culminating in the revolutionary drama of German expressionism, can
hardly be more effectively illustrated than by Georg
Kaiser's *Gas*. Uncompromising in its break with
the dramaturgical conventions of the psychological
play that had reached its perfection in the achieve-
ments of Ibsen, Kaiser's work is cast in a form
carefully calculated to convey a modern issue: it is
concerned not with the alternatives of individual
behavior but with the collective experience of a
moral crisis brought about by the consequences of
contemporary economic and technological practices.

It is not surprising that this theme should have
been stated most bluntly by the German writers
of the early twenties. A once vigorous and self-
confident society found itself disintegrating in the
wake of the defeat of 1918; and the subsequent
turmoil of political upheaval and economic collapse
created the climate for desperate outburst of
imaginative energy. Much of that expressionist
literature is utopian: it devoted itself to a scrutiny

of those human resources that might help in the rebuilding of what had been destroyed, and it turned fervently and even angrily to an analysis of those forces that seemed most inimical to a better life. But where it advanced beyond a bitter denunciation of the past, it proclaimed an image of the human being which, naive and unduly idealistic though it may seem, yet projected an order of society in which sentient and compassionate man was to be the master and not the victim of his own aspirations.

It is clear that so intense and radical a vision should excite, above all, the sensibilities of the lyrical poets, in whose work the double cry of accusation and hope can be heard again and again. But where the revolutionary message is proclaimed not merely with fervor and faith but as a challenge to be dialectically argued, it produced a curiously persuasive type of theatre. In the plays of some of these authors, lyricism and ideological convictions are often intermingled; others are less sentimental but aggressively critical of middle-class beliefs; only Georg Kaiser, an immensely productive and versatile playwright, succeeded in maintaining an artistic balance between the passion of the social revolutionary, an incorruptible eye for the logic inherent in an intellectual proposition, and the technical skill of an expert in theatre.

George Kaiser was born in Magdeburg, Germany, in 1878. As the son of a well-to-do merchant his business career seemed assured: he was sent to Argentina to work for one of the largest German power concerns, but, after three years in Buenos Aires, his health failing, he returned to Europe and lived in Italy and Spain before settling in the vicinity of Berlin. During the twenties he was the most productive of the German playwrights, and in 1930 was elected to the German Academy—a distinction of which the Nazi government deprived him four years later. Being in his social views sharply in conflict with the prevailing political climate in Germany, he emigrated to Switzerland. He continued to produce plays, fiction, and poetry. Much of his later work is not yet available in print; but it is clear that the work of his last fifteen years differs in many respects from those plays that established his reputation as an "expressionist" writer. He died in Ascona in 1945.

Kaiser's career is not easily summarized, nor has his total achievement yet received adequate critical treatment. In more than seventy plays—thirteen of them produced in 1917-18 alone—ranging from brittle comedies to savage attacks upon the delusions of his age, from modern farces to sustained tragedies in the Greek manner, he deals again and again with the forces of reason and delusion that threaten contemporary man. Kaiser is first and foremost a moralist: his theme is the "renewal of man," the search for those authentic qualities in the human being that will prove durable and creative beyond the paralysis of judgment.

Like Gerhart Hauptmann, Kaiser is a social dramatist without doctrinaire convictions; but, different from Hauptmann, he limits the scope and mobility of the individual and subjects it to the inexorable logic of circumstance and technical realities. In one of his early plays, *From Morn Till Midnight* (1916), Kaiser examines, in a series of highpitched scenes, the pathetic efforts of a bank teller who breaks out of his routine existence to find meaning and integrity. No familiar form of social life can provide it for him: he can in the end assert it only for himself. He dies a martyr in a sacrificial act of self-destruction.

Gas (1917-20) is a dramatic project of greater scope and intensity. It consists of three plays, *Die Koralle, Gas I*, and *Gas II*.

In *Die Koralle* (The Coral), the first play of this trilogy, the theme of integrity—the utopian theme of the "new man"—is elaborated in the context of an individual life: the millionaire (or, as Kaiser with characteristic over-emphasis calls him, the "billionaire") seeks in vain to cast off the haunting shadow of an unhappy childhood; he murders his double in order to obtain not only happiness but identity.

Gas I advances the argument from a private issue to a group experience: the son of the "billionaire" has become a social revolutionary, dedicated to the realization of the "new man." He offers his workers the opportunity of a humane life if they will agree to abandon the production of gas upon which the huge machinery of capitalism depends but which threatens from time to time to destroy the workers' community. At the risk of their happiness the workers prefer the "system" to "life": the new man is not yet.

For in *Gas II* (1920) the world is engulfed in apocalyptic destruction: the impact of fanatical technological thinking upon the human being is demonstrated most dramatically. The great-grandson of the billionaire is now one of the workers in a state-run plant; in an effort at preventing imminent total war he proclaims the ideals of meekness and brotherly love instead of self-ambition and battle. He fails. Not victory but the radical destruction of both warring sides is the inescapable result. The voice of the visionary cries in a wilderness of inhumanity: beyond the evidence of barbarism he can only project a dream of peace in another world.

The three plays, each artistically and intellectually complete in itself, may at first sight seem profoundly skeptical of the very idealism that constituted the chief impulse of the German expressionist poet. Yet they provide in fact the poetic elaboration, in extreme images and situations, of the economic and social implications of capitalism as Kaiser and the German revolutionary intelligentsia saw them after the First World War. The exploita-

tional character of money and the concomitant
paralysis of the individual leaves the billionaire in
The Coral with only the essentially romantic desire
for self-extinction; in *Gas I* his son proclaims an
ethical socialism which is doomed to failure in the
face of collective blindness and the compelling or
persuasive interests of the state; in *Gas II* state
socialism itself leads to a holocaust in which the
"blue figures" of capitalism and the "yellow figures"
of socialism extinguish one another. None of these
forms of economic and political organization seem
tolerable: the billionaire-worker in *Gas II* is the
"new man" who accepts the inevitable "eccentri-
city" of an absolute conviction of human integrity.
He knows that he must continue to proclaim it as
a platonic truth, an "inner realm" of meaning, to
which any future must refer.

Thus the central motif of these three plays is
the clash between a stubbornly maintained vision
of truth and the seductive and often overwhelming
compulsions of power—the power of individual satis-
faction, the power of wealth, and power in its harsh-
est and most technical modern form, exercised for
its own sake.

It is true that Kaiser insists that "the deepest
wisdom is found only by a single mind. And when
it is found it is so overwhelming that it cannot become effective." Yet, the issue which Kaiser argues
concerns all of us, it is not a private one; its moral
impact cannot therefore, as in the plays of Ibsen

and Hauptmann, be shown in a series of individual experiences with which we as spectators might identify ourselves. Indeed, Kaiser is not primarily concerned with the alternatives of action or judgment that might be open to a well-defined character; his purpose is altogether the unraveling of the implications of an intellectual position. Each turn of events, every sentence that is uttered, is, therefore, in Kaiser's plays, a key to an essentially dialectical intention. His plots are exactly developed elaborations of his central ideas. This is to say that the dramatic structure of the *Gas* trilogy is determined not so much by the logic of individual, or group, psychology, as by the logic—we might almost say, logistics—of an idea. All of Kaiser's works are masterpieces of deduction: "To write a play," Kaiser himself suggested, "is to pursue an idea to the end."

This deliberate narrowing of the dramatic intent has its striking consequences for the form of Kaiser's plays. Where intellectual and emotional tensions are to be stated with the utmost concentration a high degree of abstraction becomes inevitable. Instead of the ample and detailed setting of the naturalistic theater, Kaiser employs few but emphatic properties in an otherwise bleak and pointedly inhuman stage space. His figures are far from the psychologically plausible characters of the realistic drama; they are, rather, nameless and puppet-like cyphers, symbols of family or class relationships who are at times distinguished only by arbitrary colors and who seem to carry the argument all the more efficiently the less specific their individuality.

The same sort of reduction to a minimum of naturalness is characteristic of Kaiser's language: what is said by each of these schematic figures is tense and abrupt, and in syntax and vocabulary stripped of all leisurely irrelevancy. Whether we listen to the technical jargon of the engineer or to the anxious and more and more resolute voice of the "billionaire," we are always aware of that remarkable sense of direction with which Kaiser pursues his argument. The form of the dialogue is equally revealing: instead of justifying the actions of individual characters it seems rather to plot out the relay stations of the dramatic idea. This is perhaps nowhere more evident than in those passages where, for an extreme measure of antithetical speech, Kasier resorts to the classical device of stichomythy.

Deliberate sparseness and economy of setting, figure, and language corresponds to the precision with which the play as a whole is designed. We need only analyze with some care the fourth act of *Gas I* to recognize Kaiser's craftsmanship, his use of the fugal structure, and his skill in organizing, through sound and light and a careful manipulation of group movements, a slowly rising crescendo of urgency.

Kaiser's incomparable instinct for the theatrical effect is one of his greatest assets. Indeed, it saves his plays on the one hand from becoming mere intellectual exercises in the hands of an accomplished "Denkspieler"; and on the other from that excess of exclamatory feeling which is typical of much expressionist writing. Kaiser's passion is directed toward the illumination of rational and, therefore, arguable human alternatives; his utopian vision of the "new man" is not vague and sentimental but amounts to a calculated appraisal of the energies of heart and mind and action which the human being must marshal for his own salvation. We cannot read the final speech of the "billionaire," or the second act of *Gas II*, without being moved by the superb pathos of the moralist. Here, as in the plays of Lessing or Schiller, with whom Kaiser has in form and in substance so much in common, the work of art offers us a most articulate and compelling assertion of the humanistic faith.

VICTOR LANGE

SUGGESTED READING

Columbia Dictionary of Modern European Literature,
pp. 343-345. New York, 1947.

Diebald, B. *Der Denkspieler Georg Kaiser.* Frankfurt,
1924.

Elbe, A. M. Technische und soziale Probleme in der
Dramenstruktur Georg Kaisers, Diss. Cologne, 1959.

Fivian, E. A. *Georg Kaiser* (in German). Munich, 1946.

Frenz, H. "Georg Kaiser" in *Poet Lore* 1946, 363-369.

Freyhan, M. *Georg Kaisers Werk.* Berlin, 1926.

Fruchter, M. J. *The Social Dialectic in Georg Kaiser's
Dramatic Works.* Philadelphia, 1933.

Kenworthy, B. J. *Georg Kaiser,* 1957.

Paulsen, W. *Georg Kaiser,* 1960.

Twentieth-Century Authors, pp. 742f. New York, 1942.

GAS – II

CHARACTERS

THE BILLIONAIRE WORKER
THE CHIEF ENGINEER
FIRST
SECOND
THIRD
FOURTH } FIGURES IN BLUE
FIFTH
SIXTH
SEVENTH
FIRST
SECOND
THIRD
FOURTH } FIGURES IN YELLOW
FIFTH
SIXTH
SEVENTH

Workers: Men, Women, Old Men, Old Women,
Youths and Girls
The action takes place in the same country as that
of "Gas I," but a generation later.

2

GAS — II

ACT ONE

Concrete Hall. Light falls in dusty beams from arc-lamp. From misty height of dome dense wires horizontally to iron platform, thence diagonally distributed to small iron tables—three right, three left. Red Wires to the left, green to the right. At each table a FIGURE IN BLUE—*seated, stiffly, uniformed—gazing into glass pane in the table which, lighting up, reflects its colour on the face above it, red to the left, green to the right. Across and further down, a longer iron table chequered like a chessboard with green and red plugs—operated by the* FIRST FIGURE IN BLUE. *For a time, silence.*

SECOND FIGURE IN BLUE (*at red pane*). Report from third fighting-sector—Enemy concentration preparing.   (*Pane dark.*)

FIRST FIGURE IN BLUE (*switches red plug*).

FIFTH FIGURE IN BLUE (*at green pane*): Report from third works—production one lot below contract.   (*Pane dark.*)

FIRST FIGURE IN BLUE (*switches green plug*).

THIRD FIGURE IN BLUE (*at red pane*): Report

3

from second fighting-sector—Enemy concentration preparing. (*Pane dark.*)

FIRST FIGURE IN BLUE (*switches red plug*).

SIXTH FIGURE IN BLUE (*at green pane*): Report from second works—production one lot below contract. (*Pane dark.*)

FIRST FIGURE IN BLUE (*switches green plug*).

FOURTH FIGURE IN BLUE (*at red pane*): Report from first fighting-sector—Enemy concentration preparing. (*Pane dark.*)

FIRST FIGURE IN BLUE (*switches red plug*).

SEVENTH FIGURE IN BLUE (*at green pane*): Report from first works—production two lots below contract. (*Pane dark.*)

FIRST FIGURE IN BLUE (*switches green plug*).

(*Silence.*)

SECOND FIGURE IN BLUE (*at red pane*): Report from third fighting-sector—enemy sweeping forward. (*Pane dark.*)

FIRST FIGURE IN BLUE (*switches red plug*).

FIFTH FIGURE IN BLUE (*at green pane*): Report from third works—production three lots below contract. (*Pane dark.*)

FIRST FIGURE IN BLUE (*switches green plug*).

THIRD FIGURE IN BLUE (*at red pane*): Report from second fighting-sector—enemy sweeping forward. (*Pane dark.*)

FIRST FIGURE IN BLUE (*switches red plug*).

SIXTH FIGURE IN BLUE (*at green pane*): Report from second works—production five lots below contract. (*Pane dark.*)

FIRST FIGURE IN BLUE (*switches green plug*).

FOURTH FIGURE IN BLUE (*at red pane*): Report from first fighting-sector—enemy sweeping forward.

FIRST FIGURE IN BLUE (*switches red plug*).

SEVENTH FIGURE IN BLUE (*at green pane*): Report from third fighting-sector—enemy breaking through. (*Pane dark.*)

FIRST FIGURE IN BLUE (*switches green plug*).

(*Silence.*)

SECOND FIGURE IN BLUE (*at red pane*): Report from third fighting-sector—enemy breaking through. (*Pane dark.*)

FIRST FIGURE IN BLUE (*switches red plug*).

FIFTH FIGURE IN BLUE (*at green pane*): Report from third works—production nine lots below contract. (*Pane dark.*)

FIRST FIGURE IN BLUE (*switches green plug*).

THIRD FIGURE IN BLUE (*at red pane*): Report from second fighting-sector—enemy breaking through.

FIRST FIGURE IN BLUE (*switches red plug*).

SIXTH FIGURE IN BLUE (*at green pane*): Report

5

from second works—production eleven lots below contract. (*Pane dark.*)

FIRST FIGURE IN BLUE (*switches green plug*).

FOURTH FIGURE IN BLUE (*at red pane*): Report from first fighting-sector—enemy breaking through. (*Pane dark.*)

FIRST FIGURE IN BLUE (*switches red plug*).

SEVENTH FIGURE IN BLUE (*at green pane*): Report from first works—production twelve lots below contract. (*Pane dark.*)

FIRST FIGURE IN BLUE (*into telephone by him*): The chief engineer!

THE CHIEF ENGINEER (*comes in: aged in petrification of fanatical working energy, gaunt profile, white streak in hair, white smock*).

FIRST FIGURE IN BLUE: Control stations report less production of gas. *Is* defaults against *Must* by twelve lots.

CHIEF ENGINEER: Collapse of workers at pressure gauges, at switch-gears, at levers.

FIRST FIGURE IN BLUE: Why no substitutes?

CHIEF ENGINEER: Each shift combed of each superfluous man or woman.

FIRST FIGURE IN BLUE: Disease?

CHIEF ENGINEER: Then without visible sign.

FIRST FIGURE IN BLUE: Delivery of food unhindered?

CHIEF ENGINEER: Supply continuous, variety, plenty.

FIRST FIGURE IN BLUE: Disappointment over payment out of profits to be shared?

CHIEF ENGINEER: Already profits in net cash stuff wide even boys' pockets.

FIRST FIGURE IN BLUE: Then how do you account for . . . the discrepancy?

CHIEF ENGINEER: Movement creates its own law. Excessive repetition of single action blunts the onspurring will to work. Gas is no longer a goal—purpose vanished in the little motion which repeated and repeated became purposeless, part without whole. Planless the man at his tool—the work withdrew ever farther out of sight as the man slipped day by day ever deeper into sameness and monotony. Wheel by wheel in whirring hum yet never cogged within next wheel and next wheel. Motion roaring upwards into emptiness and, unresisted, hurtling down to earth again.

FIRST FIGURE IN BLUE: Can you discover no means by which to assure production?

CHIEF ENGINEER: New masses of workers to the machines.

FIRST FIGURE IN BLUE: Not to be found after sevenfold siftings.

CHIEF ENGINEER: Children are already on full time.

FIRST FIGURE IN BLUE: Then what?

CHIEF ENGINEER: Upleaping increase of gas deficit.

FIRST FIGURE IN BLUE (*pointing to table*): Do you see this? Calculation of attack and defence—comparison of force on either side.

CHIEF ENGINEER: Red dominates.

FIRST FIGURE IN BLUE: Enemy spreads.

CHIEF ENGINEER: Green recedes.

FIRST FIGURE IN BLUE: Gas withholds defence. (CHIEF ENGINEER *silent*.) This table works out the sum. We lack numbers, but our technical equipment is superior. That balances the outcome. So long as we maintain our technical strength. . . . With the impetus of the gas which we alone produce, our technical force far exceeds the enemy's. One lot of gas short of what is calculated here—and we lose our chance of salvation more completely than we have lost it already.

CHIEF ENGINEER (*staring*): Then the possibility of our crushing the enemy is no longer . . .?

FIRST FIGURE IN BLUE: Chimera now!

CHIEF ENGINEER: The end?

FIRST FIGURE IN BLUE: At best a draw with both sides check-mate. (CHIEF ENGINEER *catches at table for support.*) It simplifies the issue. It fell out the only possible way. Fight and downfall. Attack and resistance to the last on either side. Adversary against adversary to the last drop of blood, and they fall together. The enfeebled remnant that remains soon vanishes. None escape from that annihilation. (*strongly.*) This is knowledge only we possess!

CHIEF ENGINEER (*pulling himself together*): Then what?

FIRST FIGURE IN BLUE: Increase in production of gas without consideration of man, woman, or child. No more shifts—let one shift overlap the other without release. Every last hand mobilised from collapse to collapse. No rest, no respite. Let the last dead hand fall from the lever, the last dead foot slip off the switch-pedal, the last glazed eye turn sightless from the pressure-gauge—let this table here show: The last enemy wiped off the face of the earth, our last fighter dead at his post.

CHIEF ENGINEER (*tensely*): I will fulfill that order.

FIRST FIGURE IN BLUE (*stretching out his hand*):

9

In with us, into the tunnel that has no exit.

CHIEF ENGINEER (*taking his hand*): Gas!

(*He goes. Outside nearby, high, shrill sirens, others farther off—fainter—silence.*)

FIRST FIGURE IN BLUE (*into telephone*): The Billionaire Worker. (*he comes—middle twenties— worker's dress, shaved head, barefoot.*) Is this your shift?

BILLIONAIRE WORKER: No, but the relay summons has just sounded.

FIRST FIGURE IN BLUE: Prematurely.

BILLIONAIRE WORKER: You must have been forced into that decision.

FIRST FIGURE IN BLUE: Under what compulsion?

BILLIONAIRE WORKER: No worker can manage the earlier shift.

FIRST FIGURE IN BLUE: What is your advice?

BILLIONAIRE WORKER: What value has my advice here?

FIRST FIGURE IN BLUE: You heard—I put the question to you.

BILLIONAIRE WORKER: You can inform yourself by asking any worker in the factories.

FIRST FIGURE IN BLUE: I ask no worker—I want my information from the chief.

BILLIONAIRE WORKER: What chief?

FIRST FIGURE IN BLUE (*looking at him intently*): The one who stands before me.

BILLIONAIRE WORKER: Is this your abdication?

FIRST FIGURE IN BLUE: The new task demands redoubled strength. The chief and we unite our efforts.

BILLIONAIRE WORKER: What do you want of us?

FIRST FIGURE IN BLUE: Gas with tenfold energy.

BILLIONAIRE WORKER (*with a shrug*): You decide the production.

FIRST FIGURE IN BLUE: That does not suffice. The workers are slack. They're soft—orders would run to water in their brains instead of stiffening them to action.

BILLIONAIRE WORKER: Make your punishments harder.

FIRST FIGURE IN BLUE: And take them off their work. . . .

BILLIONAIRE WORKER: Can none be spared?

FIRST FIGURE IN BLUE: From the last great spending of our forces? No. Annihilation on both sides—but annihilation!

BILLLIONAIRE WORKER (*flinches, recovers himself*): What do you want of me?

FIRST FIGURE IN BLUE: To send through the whole works a galvanizing current. Fanaticise them

11

for the final ruin. Hate and pride can kindle a fever to heat the coldest veins for once—night will become day in the struggle to reach the goal that blood-red beacon lights.

BILLIONAIRE WORKER: Is that the goal?

FIRST FIGURE IN BLUE: Which your voice shall announce. Go amongst them in all the shops—let your words sound amidst the roar of the pistons and the hum of turning belts—overcome that din with your shout to arms that shows them the goal and lends meaning to their effort. Hands will grasp levers with new strength—feet tighten on the switch-pedals—eyes clear at the pressure-gauges. The flood-gates of work shall open wide and gas overpower power.

BILLIONAIRE WORKER (*very calm*): I am due for punishment if I miss my shift.

FIRST FIGURE IN BLUE: You are no longer a worker.

BILLIONAIRE WORKER: You have no power to dismiss any worker in this factory.

FIRST FIGURE IN BLUE: I lay you under special contract.

BILLIONAIRE WORKER: I decline to accept it.

FIRST FIGURE IN BLUE: Do you wish to make conditions?

BILLIONAIRE WORKER: I repeat the only one which is the one my mother and my mother's father demanded: Set this factory free.

FIRST FIGURE IN BLUE (*fiercely*): Your grandfather and your mother protested against the production of gas. Therefore it became necessary to use force in the works. Otherwise our preparations for this war would have come to a standstill.

BILLIONAIRE WORKER: Therefore their implacable refusal.

FIRST FIGURE IN BLUE: We are engaged in a war such as no party was ever involved in before.

BILLIONAIRE WORKER: I have obeyed every order in silence.

FIRST FIGURE IN BLUE: The time has come now for you to speak.

BILLIONAIRE WORKER: Against myself and against my mother?

FIRST FIGURE IN BLUE: For the workers who want gas. After the explosion they came back—they rebuilt the factory—they stayed in the shops in spite of danger that hourly threatened. They bowed in willingness before their master, whose name then was gas, whose name today is downfall if a voice they will heed will make it known to them. Yours

13

is that voice—at your "yes" the "yes" of thousands will light the train of fire for the ultimate destruction. Come over to us, and the half-dead will spring to life again throughout these works.

BILLIONAIRE WORKER: I defend the legacy of my grandfather.

FIRST FIGURE IN BLUE: The workers themselves laughed his plans to scorn.

BILLIONAIRE WORKER: The form for people will manifest itself.

FIRST FIGURE IN BLUE: For others who survive. There is no future for us.

BILLIONAIRE WORKER: There is always a way out.

FIRST FIGURE IN BLUE: Do you seek one without us?

BILLIONAIRE WORKER: With you and within you.

FIRST FIGURE IN BLUE (*after a moment's reflection*): We shall achieve by punishment the output we require.

>(*He makes a gesture of dismissal. The* BILLIONAIRE WORKER *goes. Silence.*)

SECOND FIGURE IN BLUE (*at red pane*): Report from third fighting-sector—enemy pressure irresistible. (*Pane dark.*)

FIRST FIGURE IN BLUE (*switches red plug*).

THIRD FIGURE IN BLUE (*at red pane*): Report

14

from second fighting-sector—enemy pressure irresistible. (*Pane dark.*)

FIRST FIGURE IN BLUE (*switches red plug*).

FOURTH FIGURE IN BLUE (*at red pane.*) Report from first fighting-sector—enemy pressure irresistible. (*Pane dark.*)

FIRST FIGURE IN BLUE (*springs up*): No report from the factories?

CHIEF ENGINEER (*enters hastily*).

CHIEF ENGINEER: Turmoil everywhere! Shift-changes hitched! Relief gang and gang on duty cease to cog! For the first time a gap opens in a system that has been flawless all the years. The pendulum swings wild! The machine has stalled.

FIRST FIGURE IN BLUE: Your organization?

CHIEF ENGINEER: Announced by sirens! Answered by the gang on duty with laying-down of tools—and by the relief-gang with ignoring it.

FIRST FIGURE IN BLUE: Is anyone inciting them to resist?

CHIEF ENGINEER: Not a wheel-minder among them! It's the machine that is running wild—and it's running wild because its works are moving to a different rhythm. The new distribution of time has disturbed the old pace and drags it down to seconds which suffice for remembrance to remember

15

themselves! Lightning flashes in heads and illuminates the path they have been driven along these years upon years! The tumult becomes a face grinning its hideousness into their horror-frozen minds!

FIRST FIGURE IN BLUE: Then — strike?

CHIEF ENGINEER: What is that?

FIRST FIGURE IN BLUE: Are they leaving switch-gear, lever, observation dial?

CHIEF ENGINEER: Already happenings of the past! Standstill turned into movement!

FIRST FIGURE IN BLUE: Commotion?

CHIEF ENGINEER: Flaming through the shops! Not a voice—not a cry—no eloquence! Silence of ice—gazing before them—or stealing a glance at the next man who does like-wise at his neighbour, and so on from partner to partner! It is out of their eyes it's coming—this thing that is on its way to shatter us to bits—this tempest!

FIRST FIGURE IN BLUE: A cordon round the shops —anyone attempting to leave to be stopped at the gates!

CHIEF ENGINEER: Is there still time?

FIFTH FIGURE IN BLUE (*at green pane*): Report from third works. . . .

CHIEF ENGINEER (*goes to him—reading off*):

16

Work stands still—workers leaving shops!

FIRST FIGURE IN BLUE: Lock the others in.

SIXTH FIGURE IN BLUE (*at green pane*): Report from second works. . . .

CHIEF ENGINEER: Work stands still. . . .

SEVENTH FIGURE IN BLUE (*at green pane.*) Report from first works. . . .

CHIEF ENGINEER: Workers leaving shops!

FIRST FIGURE IN BLUE: Alarm throughout the works!

CHIEF ENGINEER: Too late! We're crushed under the weight of their numbers. See it towering fearfully over us, the wave about to break. We have brought it towering over our heads—they come and we are here!

FIRST FIGURE IN BLUE: Are they through?

CHIEF ENGINEER: In inevitable march. The line presses back upon the place we drove them from. There the storm gathers, there, when it breaks, it shall strike us—if we are here for the striking.

FIRST FIGURE IN BLUE (*flinging the plugs together in disorder*): The calculation did not come out—there was a remainder!

(*He goes out with the* CHIEF ENGINEER *and the* FIGURES IN BLUE. *The hall remains empty. Then an ever-swelling crowd of peo-*

17

ple emerge in a circle against the dim grey walls—men young and middle-aged, old men, boys, in gray workers' clothes, shorn-headed and barefoot; women, young and middle-aged, old women, girls, in the same clothes, barefoot, with gray kerchiefs close round their hair. A short distance from the tables the dead, silent, forward-pressing, movement, stops still. The outbreak comes in a great flood—silent—yet full of haste. The tables are overturned and passed from hand to hand until they vanish into the shadowy edge of the hall; the wires from platform to tables, from dome to platform, are torn away. Then utter silence. The women pull the kerchiefs off their heads and begin to smooth their hair.)

ALL (*looking at one another—in a great shout*): No gas!

ACT TWO

Concrete hall. Dimmer light from the arc-lamps. Hall full.

VOICES (*rising clear through a murmurous swell*): What of us?

GIRL (*on the platform—spreading her hair*): Morning for us—day with a morning so filled with joy in light that it postpones the noon! Radiance streams from that morning, dawning as no morning dawned for us before. We open eyes of awe upon that wider vision, chaos of light in white and many colours . . . the wonder passes and is retrospect. Morning for me leads my lover to me by the hand.

YOUNG WORKER (*beside girl on the platform*): Morning for you and me and our fulfilment. Empty were being and seeking from day to day, neither yours nor mine until this bright morning. Now the locked waters flow once more, tide strong against the shore, riotous with colour, loud with wedding joy!

GIRL (*embracing him*): Morning for you!

YOUNG WORKER (*holding her*): Morning for you.

19

GIRLS AND YOUNG WORKERS (*pressing about the platform—embracing*): Morning for us.

VOICES OF THE OTHERS: More for us!

WOMAN (*on the platform*): Noon for us. Out of that beginning I had not yet drawn the arc that sweeps towards the height—it crept flat along the ground. Between man and wife nothing lay behind the morning—the dead husk rustled, riveting but not uniting. Now it showers out of the brightness, and the rainbow shines overhead. The clouds flaunt gold, they vanish in fire of glory the sky around, raining beneficence, warming and nourishing the dead-brittle crust. Man and wife at noon, one life, one breath, absorbed and welded, indistinguishable. Demands shall be answered, last and first, the answer rings forth with a noonday clamour through the blue noon over us.

MAN (*beside her on the platform*): Noon streams from you, driving a swarm of blue-rimmed clouds. Noon spread over me like a tent of permanence—bounding the space where I am yours. No exit to seduce where nothing serves—no will that defies where nothing signifies—the syllable is breathed and understanding outreaches further words where both command. Desire grew bold, immeasurable—body binds body, mated—our law is the doubling

20

of being and being unabated, forbidding nothing, allowing nothing, for oneness knows neither pleading nor resistance and is indivisible in Man and Woman at noon.

WOMAN (*reaching out her hands*): Noon for you!

MAN (*taking them*): Noon for you!

MEN AND WOMEN (*round the platform, seeking one another's hands*): Noon for us!

(MAN *and* WOMAN *down from platform.*)

VOICES OF OTHERS: More for us!

OLD WOMAN (*on the platform*): Evening for us. Once to be still after the day's round, feet quiet in their shoes. What were morning and noon to me? No difference to me between the noon and the morning. One and the same and all the same pattern of bitter labour, slipping by like muddy trickling water over bumps in a stream-bed we can't see the bottom of. That was morning and noon for us. . . . Was I alone? Was no one by me in the beginning and after? Was I so quite alone? Did I go under with only myself, reach out my hand only for my own other hand to save me from sinking, sinking? Had I died lonely even then? . . . Evening brings life, adding all the lost hours to the hours that shall be. Time is dealt out to a new measure—I hold out my two hands and join them about nothingness—

for it pours out of them—dazzled I look and see the treasure before me which noon and morning hid and evening reveals.

OLD MAN (*beside her on the platform*): For us the evening. Rest from the aimless, driven haste; trees and shade for us now. Where whirls the tumult? Where are they hurrying? Drowsy birds twitter in the branches—wind soughs, rustles. Day ebbs away. Is it late? Morning is forcing and crowding without peace, without end. Was there loss? The curve of a lip can extravagantly bestow. You suffered no want, I promised myself nothing—and our evening discloses a plenty we shall never exhaust. (*Leads her with him down from the platform.*)

OLD MEN AND WOMEN (*moving towards them —supporting one another*): Evening for us!

VOICES OF THE OTHERS: More for us!

A VOICE: What of us?

SOME VOICES: More for us!

OTHER VOICES: What of us?

A WAVE OF VOICES: More for us!

A COUNTER-WAVE OF VOICES: What of us?

VOICES UPON VOICES (*in flood and counter-flood*): More for us! What of us? (*Ending in a great cry. Silence.*)

A VOICE: The Billionaire Worker!

ALL THE VOICES TOGETHER (*swelling—uniting—triumphing*): The Billionaire Worker! (*Silence.*)

BILLIONAIRE WORKER (*ascends the platform*): I stand here, yours. Above you only by these steps I climb with my feet. (*On the platform.*) No mind more deep-thinking—no mouth more eloquent before you. You call to morning and to evening and to noon—and make the speakable articulate with words forever relevant. For you, Young Girl, the morning, dawn, and beginning of your life—and your sisters' here and your sisters' yet to come. That is primeval law! For you, Youth, the fire of early day, beating in blood and pulses with the first embrace—and in your brothers' here and in your brothers' yet to come. That is primeval law! For you, Woman, day big with noon, season of all fulfillment—and for all these women about you and all who are yet to come. That is primeval law! For you, Man, the high stars' brand of mighty noon—and for all these men about you and all who are yet to come. That is primeval law! For you, old men and old women, evening falling on shoulders, into laps, out of shadow and calm airs—lulling into the night that shall receive your sleep without cry, without fear. That is primeval law! (*Stronger.*)

23

Day is about you again—day and its fullness, morning and noon and evening. Law is restored and shines out from new tablets. You have come home again—out of bondage—returned to the ultimate duties of life.

VOICES: What of us?

BILLIONAIRE WORKER: Proclaim yourselves in your self-recognition—under bitterest oppression crushed to earth—penned in slavery like beasts for the slaughter—you shall be heard! Your experience shall be your seal and oath—this is no child's play. Let your cry be heard—a truth of truths—in a great YES!

VOICES UPON VOICES: What of us?

BILLIONAIRE WORKER: Report yourselves in your unfolding! Your discovery would turn to sacrilege were you to hide what you have found. Silence would set a stain upon your souls, black and terrible, never to be effaced. The air in this house of yours will turn foul if you bar your windows shut and keep that light from shining on the streets without. You would stand cursed in that instant and forever damned.

ALL THE VOICES TOGETHER: What of us?

BILLIONAIRE WORKER: Spread your tidings abroad! Send your cry forth out of this hall over all

24

the world. Spare no labour—it shall be your last. Give of your treasure: it is inexhaustible and will return tenfold. Roll the dome clear!

(*Silence.*)

VOICES UPON VOICES: Roll the dome clear!

ALL THE VOICES TOGETHER: Roll the dome clear!

BILLIONAIRE WORKER: Stretch the wire that shall flash your message around the earth's circle!

VOICES: Stretch the wire!

VOICES UPON VOICES: Stretch the wire!

ALL THE VOICES TOGETHER: Stretch the wire!

BILLIONAIRE WORKER: Send out the signal of truce to all the world's fighters!

VOICES: Send out the signal!

VOICES UPON VOICES: Send out the signal!

ALL THE VOICES TOGETHER: Send out the signal!

YOUNG WORKER (*on the platform—arms raised to the dome*): We shall clear the dome!

(*Silence.*)

VOICE (*above*): We in the dome!

VOICES (*below*): Roll the dome clear!

VOICE (*above*): Rust clogs the grooves!

VOICES (*below*): Loosen the rivets!

VOICE (*above*): Mightily pressing. . . .

VOICES (*below*): Break down the girders!

VOICE (*above*): Plates giving way!

25

VOICES (*below*): Widen the gap!

VOICE (*above*): Now the dome moves!

ALL THE VOICES TOGETHER (*below*): Roll the dome clear!

>   (*A broad beam of light falls suddenly from dome to ground, and remains there erect like a shining column. Dazzled silence—all faces raised.*)

BILLIONAIRE WORKER (*calling upward*): Speed up the work without slacking.

VOICE (*above*): The wire hangs plumb.

BILLIONAIRE WORKER: Make haste to be done.

VOICE (*above*): Wireless at summit, here in good order.

BILLIONAIRE WORKER: Flash what I call!

VOICE (*above*): We stand by.

BILLIONAIRE WORKER: Send out the rally: hands have ceased from their work—hands have quit their slaving for destruction—hands are free to take the pressure of all hands in ours which now rest. No Gas!

VOICE (*above*): Hands have ceased their work —hands are free to take the pressure of all hands in ours which now rest. No Gas!

ALL THE VOICES TOGETHER (*below*): No Gas!

BILLIONAIRE WORKER: Stand by for the answer!

26

VOICES (*below*): Tell us the answer!

(*Silence.*)

VOICE (*above*): Answer fails!

(*Silence.*)

BILLIONAIRE WORKER: Send a new call: Tumult in blood subsided—fever fell cool—sight came to eyes that look up to greet you—shift-changing turned to abidance of being—No Gas!

ALL THE VOICES TOGETHER (*below*): No Gas!

BILLIONAIRE WORKER: Watch for the answer!

VOICES UPON VOICES (*below*): Call down the answer!

BILLIONAIRE WORKER: Keep good watch for the answer!

(*Silence.*)

VOICE (*above*): Answer fails!

(*Silence.*)

BILLIONAIRE WORKER: Urge a reply: Land melted into land—frontiers into the all—the farthest are neighbours—joining with you we disperse among you, divided in oneness, one in division. No Gas!

VOICE (*above; repeating*): Land melted into land —frontiers into the all—the farthest are neighbours —joining with you we disperse among you, divided in oneness, one in division—No Gas!

ALL THE VOICES TOGETHER (*below*): No Gas!

27

BILLIONAIRE WORKER: Take the answer right!

ALL THE VOICES TOGETHER (*below*): Shout us the answer!

BILLIONAIRE WORKER: Take it up accurately to the last syllable.

(*Silence.*)

VOICE (*above*): Answer fails!

(*Dead silence.*)

VOICE (*from farthest rim of the crowd*): Strangers!

VOICES UPON VOICES: The Yellow Ones!

ALL THE VOICES TOGETHER: The Enemy!

(*They fall back, making way for seven* FIGURES IN YELLOW *who pass between them into the centre of the hall.* BILLIONAIRE WORKER *staggers from the platform.*)

FIRST FIGURE IN YELLOW: A hitch in the reckoning. A rift in the game. Yours threw the cards down, we overtrumped. Enter our losses into your books. (*Silence.*) The power of the gas you produce will serve our needs. Your work shall pay your debt but never liquidate it. Gas is our fuel. (*Silence.*) The works pass from your disposal to our commands. We scrap the schedule of your sharings. Proceeds shall concentrate out of your many hands into our few—wages for you in the minimum meas-

28

ure for maintenance of strength. (*Silence.*) From this hour these works resume the production of gas. You entered this hall as a crowd, you leave it as shifts—back to your service, shift succeeding shift. We are the users of gas and demand it—the Chief Engineer is the maker of gas and shall answer to us. (CHIEF ENGINEER *comes.*) The Chief Engineer stands in power over you to order and punish. (*Silence. To the* CHIEF ENGINEER.) Set the hall to rights.

CHIEF ENGINEER (*calls upwards*): Roll the dome shut. (*The sunlight diminishes and is gone.*) Set up the tables. (*With noiseless and rapid obedience tables are reached over the heads of the crowd and set up in the centre.*) Stretch the wires. (*Swiftly, dully, wires are stretched from where they hang perpendicular from the dome diagonally to the tables as before.*) Recharge the lamps. (*Dusty light-beams from arc-lamps.*) To the shops, forward! (*Wordless melting away towards the edge of the hall—vanishment.*)

(SIx FIGURES IN YELLOW *sit down at the tables.* FIRST FIGURE IN YELLOW *arranges the plugs at the switch-board.* CHIEF ENGINEER *waits.*)

FIRST FIGURE IN YELLOW (*to the* CHIEF ENGINEER). Gas! (CHIEF ENGINEER *off.*)

29

ACT THREE

Cement hall. Dusty light beams from arc-lamp. At the tables the secen FIGURES IN YELLOW. *Silence.*

SECOND FIGURE IN YELLOW (*at red pane*): Report from requisitions headquarters—two quotas more required for third district.　　(*Pane dark.*)

FIRST FIGURE IN YELLOW (*switches red plug*).

FIFTH FIGURE IN YELLOW (*at green pane*): Report from third works: Production one lot below contract.　　　　　　　　(*Pane dark.*)

FIRST FIGURE IN YELLOW (*switches green plug*).

THIRD FIGURE IN YELLOW (*at red pane*): Report from requisitions headquarters: Three quotas more required for second district.　　(*Pane dark.*)

FIRST FIGURE IN YELLOW (*switches red plug*).

SIXTH FIGURE IN YELLOW (*at green pane*): Report from second works: Production one lot below contract.　　　　　　　(*Pane dark.*)

FIRST FIGURE IN YELLOW (*switches green plug*).

FOURTH FIGURE IN YELLOW (*at red pane*): Report from requisitions headquarters: Four quotas more required for first district.　　(*Pane dark.*)

FIRST FIGURE IN YELLOW (*switches red plug*).

SEVENTH FIGURE IN YELLOW (*at green pane*): Report from first works: Production two lots under contract. (*Pane dark.*)

FIRST FIGURE IN YELLOW (*switches green plug*). (*Silence.*)

SECOND FIGURE IN YELLOW (*at red pane*): Report from requisitions headquarters: Five quotas more required for third district. (*Pane dark.*)

FIRST FIGURE IN YELLOW (*switches red plug*).

FIFTH FIGURE IN YELLOW (*at green pane*): Report from third works: Production six lots under contract. (*Pane dark.*)

FIRST FIGURE IN YELLOW (*switches green plug*).

THIRD FIGURE IN YELLOW (*at red pane*): Report from requisitions headquarters: Eight quotas more required for second district. (*Pane dark.*)

FIRST FIGURE IN YELLOW (*switches red plug*).

SIXTH FIGURE IN YELLOW (*at green pane*): Report from second works: Production ten lots under contract. (*Pane dark.*)

FIRST FIGURE IN YELLOW (*switches green plug*).

FOURTH FIGURE IN YELLOW (*at red pane*): Report from requisitions headquarters: Eleven quotas more required for first district. (*Pane dark.*)

FIRST FIGURE IN YELLOW (*switches red plug*).

31

SEVENTH FIGURE IN YELLOW (*at green pane*): Report from first works: Production twelve lots under contract. (*Pane dark.*)

FIRST FIGURE IN YELLOW (*springs up—telephones*): The Chief Engineer! (CHIEF ENGINEER *comes—without haste*): Check-up stations; verify decreased production of gas. *Is* defaults against *Must* by twelve lots.

CHIEF ENGINEER (*calmly*): Are you astonished?

FIRST FIGURE IN YELLOW: Does personal opinion enter?

CHIEF ENGINEER (*shrugging shoulders*): If you can deny yourself.

FIRST FIGURE IN YELLOW: Automaton as all are here.

CHIEF ENGINEER: The automata in the shops are moving fast with accessory sounds.

FIRST FIGURE IN YELLOW: Buzzing what?

CHIEF ENGINEER: "Not for me."

FIRST FIGURE IN YELLOW: Meaning?

CHIEF ENGINEER: This hand lifting lever—not for me. This foot pressing switch-pedal—not for me. These eyes watching pressure-gauge—not for me.

FIRST FIGURE IN YELLOW: Do you know your responsibility?

32

CHIEF ENGINEER: Gas.

FIRST FIGURE IN YELLOWS You will be held to account for every minus in delivery.

CHIEF ENGINEER (*peculiarly*): I am prepared —for the reckoning.

FIRST FIGURE IN YELLOW: You applied your powers?

CHIEF ENGINEER (*as before*): Not yet.

FIRST FIGURE IN YELLOW: You inflicted no punishments?

CHIEF ENGINEER: Upon whom?

FIRST FIGURE IN YELLOW: The hand that falters at the lever—the foot that misses the switch-pedal —the eyes that blink before the pressure-gauge.

CHIEF ENGINEER: And take every man, woman and child off the shift.

FIRST FIGURE IN YELLOW: All resisting?

CHIEF ENGINEER: We weaken from shift to shift.

FIRST FIGURE IN YELLOW: Then what next?

CHIEF ENGINEER: Gas!

FIRST FIGURE IN YELLOW: Why did you not flog the first that flagged?

CHIEF ENGINEER: No.

FIRST FIGURE IN YELLOW: Did you doubt its spread, having begun?

CHIEF ENGINEER: No.

33

FIRST FIGURE IN YELLOW: Why did you conceal these occurrences?

CHIEF ENGINEER: I did so.

FIRST FIGURE IN YELLOW: Are you supporting the revolt?

CHIEF ENGINEER: With all my power.

FIFTH FIGURE IN YELLOW (*at green pane*): Report from third works: Production . . .

CHIEF ENGINEER (*triumphantly*): Stopped!

SIXTH FIGURE IN YELLOW (*at green pane*): Report from first works: Production . . .

CHIIEF ENGINEER: Stopped!

(The FIGURES IN YELLOW *leave their tables.*)

FIRST FIGURE IN YELLOW: Who . . .?

CHIEF ENGINEER: My orders! As I left to come here. With my power behind them, conferred by yourself. The obedient obey. No more hands lifting levers—for others. No more feet pressing switch-pedals—for others. No more eyes watching pressure-gauges—for others. Hand falls, fist clenches against you—foot withdraws, poises to run against you—eyes turn away, dart glances against you. Gas for us—gas against you!

FIRST FIGURE IN YELLOW: Do you overlook the consequences?

CHIEF ENGINEER: None for us.

34

FIRST FIGURE IN YELLOW: Batteries surround the works.

CHIEF ENGINEER: In triple circle.

FIRST FIGURE IN YELLOW: Primed for the first sign of rebellion.

CHIEF ENGINEER: Rebellion rages!

FIRST FIGURE IN YELLOW: The works to the last man, into the dust with one volley.

CHIEF ENGINEER: Are you sure?

FIRST FIGURE IN YELLOW: We await your report of resumption of work within minimum delay. (*He signs to the* FIGURES IN YELLOW—*they leave together.*)

CHIEF ENGINEER (*at front table—telephones*): Leave all shops—meeting in the hall.

(*Crowd entrance—shoving accumulation towards centre—full hall.*)

VOICE (*at last—shrill, frightened*): Who has turned us off?

CHIEF ENGINEER: Those who fill this place with crowding pressure to limit of its walls. Those who left lever, switch-block, and gauge-glass in the lurch. Those who were serf-silence and will now be freemen-voice.

VOICES UPON VOICES: Who has turned us off?

CHIEF ENGINEER: Those whose hands double to

35

fists defying. Those whose feet rush to the attack. Those whose eyes take in the measure of the slave-master.

ALL THE VOICES TOGETHER: Who has turned us off?

CHIEF ENGINEER: Your command is your destiny. Your word is your law. Yesterday, rented slaves—masters today.

(*Silence.*)

VOICE: What of us?

CHIEF ENGINEER: Release from debt and deeper debt. Backs pull straight after burden and yoke. Strangling compulsion relaxed.

VOICES UPON VOICES: What of us?

CHIEF ENGINEER: Up from the knees. Weakness grows strong. Fear soars to fight.

ALL THE VOICES TOGETHER: What of us?

CHIEF ENGINEER: Unleash the slinking rage in you. Unleash the hatred that cringed in you. Unleash the poison that oozed in you. Repay!

VOICES: Have we power?

CHIEF ENGINEER: Pushed from shadow into light. Purple for your rags. Nothingness raised to affluence.

VOICES UPON VOICES: Have we power?

CHIEF ENGINEER: Beyond all measure. No

36

weapon can strike with the force of your arms raised to strike. No shot is deadlier than the breath of your lungs. You are on the march, conquerors, before ever you reach the field.

ALL THE VOICES TOGETHER: Have we power?

CHIEF ENGINEER: The battle is yours without the loss of a knuckle-joint. In less than half a day, the day is yours. Where is the means to victory more terrible than yours? Poison Gas! (*He takes a red globe out of his pocket.*) My discovery for you. Beasts of burden you, and I too—and the shame devoured me for all of us. Not for a second did I lose sight of my goal, to destroy our whip-masters—at last I reached it—the formula that frees: hatred and shame were its ingredients. In a skin-thin glass—victory: that swells and eats away flesh from legs, bleaches stiff bones. (*Silence.*) There is no looking on the power of annihilation with impunity. Reason leaves, and madness enters the brain of the beholder who sees living men turned to bleached skeletons before his very eyes. Resistance screams itself down out of the mouth of the first inquisitive one who rashly rushes hither, crying out world's end and massacre! (*Silence.*) This is the decisive hour for time everlasting—decide, and you are the victors. Set the example—

hurl your ball from the top of the dome—aim at the lines waiting to aim at you—meet onslaught with onslaught— hurl your balls!

VOICES: Poison gas.

CHIEF ENGINEER: Be avengers!

VOICES UPON VOICES: Poison gas!

CHIEF ENGINEER: Be fighters!

ALL THE VOICES TOGETHER: Poison gas!

CHIEF ENGINEER: Be conquerors!

(*Young workers crowd on to the steps of the platform—hands out-stretched for the globe.* BILLIONAIRE WORKER *pushes his way through them past their uplifted arms.*)

BILLIONAIRE WORKER: Don't touch that globe. Reject that temptation. Do not destroy your power with the hurling of the balls.

VOICES: The Billionaire Worker!

BILLIONAIRE WORKER: Do not follow those orders. Do not aim in the dark. Do no mean and paltry trafficking.

VOICES UPON VOICES: The Billionaire Worker!

BILLIONAIRE WORKER: Protect your privileges. Know your means of conquest. Build upon rock the house that shall stand unshaken forever.

ALL THE VOICES TOGETHER: The Billionaire Worker!

(*The young workers have fallen away from the steps. The* BILLIONAIRE WORKER *ascends further.*)

BILLIONAIRE WORKER: Spread your sight to span the new that began in the old. Beginning meets end, new truth, truth revealed. All ages debouch in your age, endlessly repeating. Your need is not discovery—your fulfillment not experiment and proof. Your lot is in the wheel thousands of years revolving—purifying your decisions with sorting and sorting. (*Silence.*) No road of many turnings leads to perfection as the street that is opening for you now. Yours the gain—your tables ran over. Riches were piled up all round you. (*Silence.*) But it scattered away like sand children play with on the beach. The rising of a wind retards nothing—you cannot stop springs black with the birth of earth-disturbing tempest. Momentum of release met you and flung you to the ground. A deep fall. The tower of your own height buried you. (*Silence.*) You were reckoned great before—you shall be greater now—as martyrs. (*Silence.*) The unslaked passion left you—day-labour. Endlessly satiating the nameless other replaced it. Not tables and shifts and dismissals feed it; but its own coin that pays never more, never less. (*Silence.*) Pay with the

39

counterfeit they demand of you. Cheat the cheater with his own spurious currency's dull ring. Your work brings nothing to maturity—do it. Their currency is falling—convert it. Martyrs in the works —freemen in yourselves. (*Silence.*) Build up the kingdom. Not with the burden of new discoveries —distance does not intimidate. Hard upon the ungrudging promise crowd the first-fruits—law long and long since, piled on law—preparations ripe, time out of mind—use your existence to which all reverts —build to the last stronghold the kingdom which is in yourselves. (*Silence. The* BILLIONAIRE WORKER *on the platform.*) You shall dare what generations and generations have bred in you. You exiled one of yourselves, and wisely—over green pastures he decoyed you here before me. Not from outside can you protect the greatness within you—you cannot pen it in with colony and colony—your kingdom is not of this world! (*Silence.*) Face the stranger —pay him his interest—leave him his wage—shovel him his gains—suffer his demands—ignore the spine bleeding in your skin—Be your Kingdom! (*Breathing silence.*)

CHIEF ENGINEER (*at the foot of the steps*): Treachery spits in your faces in that cry—do you not hear it? Have you no tongues to downcry it?

40

Have you forgotten the pledge of your surging voices raised to me?

BILLIONAIRE WORKER: Deliver yourselves within yourselves!

CHIEF ENGINEER: What will remain to you once dispossessed? Your necks for the bloody spurring of the lash—yourselves for defilement, laughing you to scorn—a cattle-team misused. And drudgery for ever, a whimgin cranking you eternally round and round, wearing and bearing you down. To be racked with chastisement when your limbs break under you. Those are your terms of hire.

BILLIONAIRE WORKER: Let the kingdom arise, which shall reign in you almighty.

CHIEF ENGINEER: Let the power fall low which exploits you now. Yours the gain—without the bending of a finger. Gas the magician works for you. You use your victory as the victors of yesterday showed you to.

BILLIONAIRE WORKER: Deliver yourselves in the endurance of serfdom which cannot touch the kingdom within.

CHIEF ENGINEER: Think of the tribute that will fall to you. No place on the world's globe but will be your debtor, no ships hold but will carry freight for you, no bridge but whose arch bears supplies

41

for you, no wire but flashes your commands from pole to pole. Your will is world-empire.

BILLIONAIRE WORKER: The voice speaks again —the light that tempts and dazzles shines out again.

CHIEF ENGINEER: Give your purpose voice that it may bind you implacably.

BILLIONAIRE WORKER: Decide for the way of humility.

CHIEF ENGINEER: Strike a bargain with your term and the bombardment!

BILLIONAIRE WORKER: Return to your places, perform your services—they are the lesser part.

CHIEF ENGINEER (*on the platform*): Take aim and cast the single throw which gives you victory.

BILLIONAIRE WORKER: Return!

CHIEF ENGINEER (*holding the globe high*). Dominion!

BILLIONAIRE WORKER: Found the kingdom!

CHIEF ENGINEER: Ignite the gas that kills!

(*Silence.*)

BILLIONAIRE WORKER: Be silent and listen how heaven and earth both hold their breath before your decision which shall seal the fate of the world.

(*Silence.*)

VOICES: The gas that kills!

VOICES UPON VOICES: The gas that kills!

ALL THE VOICES TOGETHER: The gas that kills!

CHIEF ENGINEER (*victorious*): Ours the power! Ours the world! Aim the bomb—hasten the throw —they shall not shoot! . . . Who volunteers?

YOUNG WORKERS (*storming on to the platform*): I!

CHIEF ENGINEER: Have a care of this ball—it is dangerous.

BILLIONAIRE WORKER (*restraining the young workers—turning to the* CHIEF ENGINEER): I am the rightful one—I have priority.

ALL THE VOICES TOGETHER: The Billionaire Worker! (*The* CHIEF ENGINEER *gives him the bomb.*)

BILLIONAIRE WORKER (*on the platform—bomb upraised over his head*). My blood's blood beat for our conversion. My thirst slaked itself at the thirst of mother and mother's father. Our voices might have waked the wilderness—Our voices could wake the wilderness—men's ears are deaf. I am vindicated! I can fulfill! (*He throws the bomb into the air— it falls and smashes with a frail clatter. Silence.*)

CHIEF ENGINEER: The gas that kills.

ALL THE VOICES: The gas that kills.

(*Paralysed silence. Bombardment thunders from without. Darkness, and vast crash of*

collapsing walls. Silence. Light comes grad-
ually. The hall a shambles of cement slabs
lying on top of one another like broken
gravestones—the skeletons of the workers
already bleached jut out amongst them.
Figure in Yellow—*helmeted, telephone at*
head, hastens towards the wreckage, un-
rolling wire.)

Figure in Yellow (*stops—stares wildly—shrieks*
into telephone): Report of effect of bombardment
—Turn your bullets on yourselves—exterminate
yourselves—the dead crowd out of their graves—
day of judgment—*dies irae—solvet—in favil. . . .*

(*His shot shatters the rest. In the mist-grey*
distance sheaves of flaming bombs bursting together
—vivid in self-extermination.)

THE END

44